THE UNGENDERED

*

Poetry Journal

Delia .M. Watterson

Mwanaka Media and Publishing Pvt Ltd,
Chitungwiza Zimbabwe

*

Creativity, Wisdom and Beauty
Publisher:

Mmap

Mwanaka Media and Publishing Pvt Ltd

24 Svosve Road, Zengeza 1

Chitungwiza Zimbabwe

mwanaka@yahoo.com

https//mwanakamediaandpublishing.weebly.com

Distributed in and outside N. America by African Books Collective

orders@africanbookscollective.com

www.africanbookscollective.com

ISBN:978-1-77906-359-5

EAN: 9781779063595

DISCLAIMER

All views expressed in this publication are those of the author and do not necessarily reflect the views of *Mmap*.

Table of Contents

Introduction

When I started writing I was thirteen years old; I would make anonymous submissions to the school magazine of the High school I attended. I never felt confident enough to publish under my own name because I was always comparing myself to everyone else. I also grew up in a family where writing was not considered a feasible profession, and any mention of it would result in screaming and possible violence.

My father was one of the people that persistently battered my spirit growing up, a year before he died I decided to publish a poetry journal and life came along and deflated my confidence to publish it, I decided to test the waters before I committed and submitted my poetry to an online poetry site.

I found it strange, but, a very kind man Alan Horwitz published one of my poems almost a year later; *The Beast with Two Backs,* it was my synopsis on life to date, and that was; a manipulative fuck and the coercion into it. Since then I have had the pleasure of being included in a few other poetry publications due to Tendai Mwanaka; *Best New African Poets 2015, Experimental Writing Volume 1* and of course he is the publisher of this poetry book; experimental writing and lyrical prose journal.

I work in finance and as someone who has grown up in an environment where you are constantly expected to climb in a box and fall in line; I appreciate and respect those that don't. Many people in the world have grown up dysfunctional, have grown up conditioned and chained up by expectations, stereotypes, responsibilities and beliefs that have limited them. In a world that is constantly changing; we have to learn to change with it, while keeping what matters, as close to us, and as dear to us, as it always has been.

This journal is dedicated to those and to my daughters.

Jade and Cas; I love you both, don't let anyone break your spirit and never lose your loving hearts and natures.

*

The content of this journal is of an adult nature, it is strongly advised that those easily offended should not read it. The author will not be held liable for any damage due to advisory.

Open your eyes and broaden the close mindedness.

Asphalt playground

Children playing,
in an asphalt playground,
folding paper planes,
out of scrap paper found.
Children lying on the asphalt now,
scarlet curtains,
fluttering out of a sad home's eyes,
dark eyes looking up at mom's house.

Asphalt playground,
With cow bones scattered about,
Eyes high up,
On a children's playground.
Used condoms and ear buds,
Stale bread and infestations of pigeons,
Broken gates,
Twisted metal promising tetanus.

Bye! The children call out,
Bye! They chorus and shout.
On an asphalt playground.

The Death Star

Beacon and mast,
The death star.
Star to the wandering,
Star to the lost.
The death star,
Star to the dead,
Light to the darkened,
Love to the frightened.

The glow upon the ancient walls,
A hand that scribed the scrolls.
The death star,
The sun in the sky;
the star dying.

Painted Sleeves

Bruised lips crushed against,
Your taste.
Hair pulled back,
Throat exposed,
Pulsing vein.

Rough hands,
Painted sleeves,
Holding, wanting,
Heart beating,
against a chest,
Breath rasping,
Bodies wet with sweat.

Perfected love and hate,
Perfect recoil and grip,
Painted sleeves,
The name,
the desire,
the bullet.

Mother

Clawing deep into the flesh,
Dragging back and lifting,
dropped by the wayside,
returning to dig deep again.
Another dig, deeper than before,
snapping and breaking,
like tendons and bones.

Beneath the surface.
Who hears the cry out of pain?
Beneath the surface is mayhem,
Levels shifting to hold together,
Plates shaking and fracking,
Steal screaming and bending like broken backs,
Erosion and landslides destroying pegs holding earth back.
Foundations and riggings weakened to collapse.

Above the surface it carries on,
The bowels of the earth ignored,
Drowned out by machine,
The earth grumbles,
The earth groans,
The earth cries out beneath;
And our Mother moans.

SMILE

Upon lips,
the sweetest,
A synergy burning wild,
waves beneath a look of calm.
Growing like a seedling in the desert sun.
Spring sunshine, warm,
melts the snow,
Eyes glowing,
alight with awe and woe.

Beauty of the green hills,
Wonder at the pure blue sky,
A breeze that bends the daffodils,
And scatters them flying.
The scent of manna and ambrosia,
upon the winds like a kiss,
The simple flutter of a butterfly's wings.

Tears fall from heavy clouds,
joy rolls down hilly cheeks,
crying relief out loud,
sobbing its heartache down,
pouring it onto,
the scorched,
the cracked,
and the parched.

Smile and wonder,
Cry and laugh,
The sun,
The rain,
The earth.

ALL-SORTS KID

A handful of sleep and alert,
A handful of all sorts,
Eyes wide, cotton mouth,
Hands trembling all the time,
all-sorts kid am I,
A handful of buzzing high,
all-sorts kid,
all-sorts death wish.

Before you start your day,
Take an all-sorts, hey!
Before you make your way,
Take and follow the all-sorts way!
buzzing you to death,
all-sorts kid,
Cotton mouth, anxious kid,
all-sorts, hey,
all-sorts death wish.

Eyes glazed, all sorts haze,
all sorts kid of today,
Hey, hey, hey,
Shaking hands, all sort buzz,
I don't know what they say'
Hey, hey, hey,
Everyone is cray-zzzz,

all sorts kid of today,

Can't think, can't blink,
all-sorts kid,
Hey, hey, in a haze.
Can't be, can't dream,
all sorts kid,
Hey, hey, in a haze,
Take another, take another,
Listen to what the doctors say,
all sorts kid of today.

Insomniac, with anxious mind,
Hamster wheeling all the time,
all sorts kid of today.
Appetite suppressed,
Looks good in a dress,
all sorts kid of today,
all sorts, hey, hey, hey
with your mind;
you pay.

Love?

Put down your gun's love,
Put down your fists,
Put down your doubled standards.
No love carries arms,
And no action of Love places guns,
Into the hands of anyone.
Let your women and children free Love,
They tire of hiding their tears,
Of been unworthy and unclean.
Let them free love,
They deserve to be heard and seen.
Let them free love,
Love doesn't cause tears and fears.

Love? Why are you threatening?
حب ? You claim peace and love?
Jacayl? Why are your women and children bleeding?
Ibig? Why are your women and children screaming?
Amour? Why are your women and children not dreaming?
Rudo? Why are your women and children starving still?
Любовь ? Why are your women sold off to pigs?
Liebe? How many daughters cry to you daily?
愛 ? Why are your women still traded into sex slavery?
אַהֲבָה ? Why are daughters crying around the world?
Why Love?

Love; put down your guns,
Love put down your fists,
Put them down to rest,
For the women and children,
Pleading, dying and bleeding,
For Love to begin.

The ankh

Man and woman,
One and whole;
The mark of the ungendered soul.
The misinterpreted angel,
Looping, to hold;
The ancient,
The temple,
An ungendered soul.
Marked by angels,
The ankh as you know,
The truth;
Of an Angel,
Which made earth a home.
Surrounded in prayer,
Surrounded by old,
Surrounded by Angels,
By the ungendered souls.

You never, now see

A face,
age.
Easy,
Desperate grace.
A naughty grin,
Eyes that spell bedroom sins.

You never see;
The grotesque,
The hidden deep,
Starving it daily, to keep it within.
The torn stiches.
Fists stuffed in a mouth,
Stopping cry's from coming out.
Suppressed pain;
That you never see.

You see;
The glint of a magnetic card strip.
Gold glowing in eyes dark and deep.
What you take and get away with.

Now see.

Scattered thoughts

Blisters oozing,
Bleeding down a back,
A loosened screw
Up and down again.
What do I have to do?
To smile again?

From lonely;
To another,
Let's not go down this road again,
It's all been said,
Man have I eaten and fed.
What do I have to do?
How do I prove it?
How do I do it?

With all these words in my head,
With all these verses up these stairs.

Scattered thoughts;
No way of doing it.
Peace to win,
Wanting peace within.

Desire

Biting kisses,
Clawing nails,
Red welts,
Leaving stinging trails.

Rough beard,
Grazing flesh,
Rough hands,
Around my neck.

Hair loose,
And falling free,
Handfuls grabbed,
And pulled smartly.

Eyes burning,
Belly aflame within,
A harsh fire,
Aching, moaning, calling.

Again, and again.

Heart

Stop beating;
Do what is threatening,
I can't survive.

Embryonic; you and I,
With all the fights,
Stairs,
And black eyes.

The drugs upon my arrival,
Chasing us on,
While bringing us down.

Stop beating;
Before torn out,
By another liar,
With a shallow heart.
Stop beating;
We will never survive.
Stop beating;
Burst from my chest,
Before its torn from us by jest.

Stop beating;
Just stop, no more,
Stop beating,

Beat no more,
Stop beating;
The last beat for.

Whisper roughly

Whisper roughly;
While you love me,
Gently graze,
Your mouth and fingers,
In the places I love;
Linger.

Whisper roughly;
As you cup me,
Hold my hips above you,
Slowly, lowering,
On to you.

Whisper roughly;
As you thrust into me,
Touching my skin,
My body, all my sins.

Whisper roughly;
Fuck me.

Black or White

I don't know,
What it is like,
To be,
Black or white.

White;
a color,
that is,
and isn't,
technically;
a color,
reflecting all,
like prisms of light.

I don't know;
What it is like,
To be,
Black or white.

Black;
A color,
That is,
And isn't,
Technically,
A color,
Absorbing all,

Holding all in the night.

Both;
In balance,
Color of light,
And darkness,
The color of night;
The color of twilight.

One day

Sky was blue again,
Sullen,
Miserable and grey,
Moody and threatening,
To cry the whole day.

Moon had hurt sky,
By leaving early,
And arriving late,
And wouldn't leave stars to play,
And went by the sea to stay.

Sun tried to console sky,
But sky said;

"Moon is too late,
I won't accept the sorry moon will say."

Sun smiled and dried sky's tears,
and the wind whispered;

"you will, one day,
And one day;
is not too late."

Regret

Your name wept,
And spat at,
Pierced chest,
Dagger after dagger sent.

Regret;
Your stench,
Makes me wretch,
Dry heaving,
Heaving up despise.

Regret; we all lost,
We paid the cost,
The cost we all pay,
A piece of soul,
A piece of heart;
To find a way,
Way to escape;
Regret.

Where are we now?

This place;
This place of boxes;
A place of mirrors,
A place of lost things.
This place of pain,
This place of sorrow,
This place invisible to outside;
A place of horror.
This place of savagery;
This place of mercenaries,
This place;
The place of no tomorrow.

This place;
The place,
The place of fallen.
The earth is what we call it.
This place;
Once a place;
A place of promise.

Peace

I will have a piece of that,
A big fat chunk that I don't have to pay back,
No one will know, if I just take that.
It will affect no one,
No one will see death crept in.

It's just a piece,
It's just what I need,
Its what's owed to me!
It's a Piece, it's a peace,
It's a piece of nothing, about Peace.
That starts with a piece.

The Piano keys

Haunting is your voice,
Tiresome are your scales,
To climb those scales,
And hold the notes in key,
You exhaust me.

Ascending and descending,
The somber yet beautiful melody,
The playing of the keys,
The keys walked in sleep.
The notes held struggling.

THE EYES OF ARMAGEDDON

look into eyes of extinction,
see America in pieces,
a missile Mrs.,
see center', - center less.

see religion as the cause of it,
see two retaliators on either side of it,
see technology and machinery as the base plate,
see humanity will never be the same again.

see deformed children,
see baron earth,
see rockets leaving,
see a symbol lowly,
see the center of it all.

see mining and hard hats,
under foot,
numbers and codes,
mushroom clouds,
that leave behind skulls.

Addict

Dilated eyes strained wide;
Trying to convince mine,
That yours are truthful, not filled with lies.

Was this your promise?
This before me,
So high and so low?

Are these the sons of tomorrow?
The ragged dressed in taters;
Chewing on bottom lips, hands agitated?

Corner curb, leaned up lamppost,
A bend in the knee of a nomad,
A tilt in his look, says yes.

Trembling voice, yearning a hit,
Hands that fidget,
Eyes that are scanning what you can get at.

The look of addict.

Dream

You sing a soul song to me,
One about happiness,
One about bliss,
About lovers wrapped in passionate kisses,

Breathe in my desolate,
Embrace my soul neglect,
Love my broken wings,
And turn it with Magic.

Into something beautiful,
Into something useful.

Dream;
Dream for me your dream.

Vanity's crotch

A Lying puckered faced bitch;
Vanity's crotch,
Thick with lipstick.

Place a butterfly blind on eyes that cannot see,
Painted lips to match her ruby heart of greed,

Lies a ream; lies like disease,

Kissing air kisses.
a kiss on each cheek;
Smiling a smile hiding,
the guilt chewed between teeth,

A Lying puckered faced bitch;
Vanity's crotch,
Thick with lipstick.

A prayer to father time;

Father time of mine,
Take my hand and walk me down,
Walk me to the edge where all I need is to fall,
Fall over and down into the abyss of a cavernous world.
Down the corridors with locks and keys,
Swinging and dangling from a chain clipped to jeans.
The doors of time and memory,
Hidden and locked because no one believes,
The love, the pain, the desolation,
The sins, the disgraces,
None of them my loose lipped shames,
I did not disclose the roses,
A viperous asp close to a breast did,
Enemy kept close, too close, took my last breath.

Love; I don't know you,

I would remember it; I am sure of it.

Love if you come, you won't know who I am,
You don't know me,

We have never danced,
We have never laughed.

Love; I know your counterpart;
It is your counterpart that mangled my heart.

Tablets, taxis, trails.

Tablets, taxis, trails;
Icon swiped, finger hold.
Neat pigtails that sit,
swiping icons on a desktop,
Hello Kitty bag hanging on a chair.

Tablets, taxis, trails;
Dust in a face, coughing tb,
Torn old vest upon a chest,
Standing in the cold outside a rural clinic,
"umama, umama, umama." Crying alone.

Tablets, taxis, trails;
Air-conditioned boxes in a row,
White garden fences,
Astroturf and plastic flowers,
Iron swing in a garden.

Tablets, taxis, trails;
Fighting township dogs,
overturned bins,
mothers with breasts that will never feed,
string tied to wild monkeys caught, food to eat.

Tablets, taxis, trails;
Skipping along manicured lawns,

31

Shiny shoes sitting in a restaurant,
Trained hands holding chopsticks with sushi,
Bowls of rice and steamed vegetables.

Tablets, Taxis, trails;
Shoeless, dirty feet walking a dirt road,
Carrying buckets of dirty water,
Sacks of meal upon shoulders,
Robbed before he reaches home.

Tablets, taxis, trails;
Kiss upon a forehead,
Night lamp turned on next to a bed,
LED butterfly mobile above a head,
Sweet dreams to bed.

Tablets, taxis, trails;
Mother screaming from a drunken blow,
Father pulling child up from the mat on the floor,
Kicking another to make room for them all,
Wind and cold coming through a shanty door.

Tablets, taxis, trails;
Tablets, taxis, trails,
Tablets, taxis, trails,
Tablets, taxis, trails.

Philippine princess

Philippine princess with pinked cheeks,
Cheap lip gloss and mini dress,
Dark hair falling upon a drunken tourist,
Smiling and talking sweetly to him.
Eyes glinting,
the reflection of a Rolex on an arm,
sunset sets the surprise,
she is not interested in the bulge between his thighs.
Philippine Princess with swift fingers,
Pretend to undress,
Let the straps fall from shoulders he caresses,
Slip a hand into a pocket,
Laugh girlishly at him stumbling in hotel bushes,
Top up his glass,
He holds a hand over the glass, enough,
Laughing she pushes his hand aside,
All the way to the top laughing,
Pushes her to the bed groping,
Then he finds it,
Shout of violence,
A boy girl in a dress,
A beautiful Philippine princess.

Clandestine Korea

Clandestine Korea;
Stoic burp of air force;
Nuclear words,
Short man from birth,
your temper is unkempt within its girth.
Clandestine Korea;
Coal mines worth,
Young girls worth two dollars,
Little boys digging from five,
Rifle in hands.

Clandestine Korea;
Put your dick away,
We know what you have,
You don't need to say,
Clandestine Korea,
Mind your way,
You anger many,
They will shoot first before they play.

The fall,

The wall,
Demons and angels,
Fables and myths,
Gathering on the field,
Swords drawn,
Shields worn,
The battle line drawn,
Screaming running at each other,
Jumping, slicing, slaying,
Bloody corpses,
Massacred faces,
Merciless hatred versus righteousness.

The riders swoop in on dragon's fire,
Burning all and everything.
The angels blow the trumpets,
The demons snarl with bloodied teeth,
The fables and the myths stand as archers,
Arrows drawn and aimed at the heart of;

The beast.

Earths Angels

Imagine you were the impossible;
The mythical;
The unbelievable,
The incomparable;

An ungendered soul,
An Earth Angel.

Would you;
Make yourself known?
Would you tell of what you feel?
guide those seeking?
Help,
inspire people?

Imagine if you held in your hands;
ideas dead and dying;
beings,
afraid of their lives lead,
Of who they meet in the end.

Imagine if you sat listening to those crying;
Those you know are hiding,
those who give up,
beaten through trying.

Imagine a being;
Just like you or them,
A soul in disguise,
Avoiding human despise.

Could you Imagine?
Could you Watch it all?
Never getting involved?
Judging what you don't know.

Imagine you are benevolence;
Neither masculine,
Nor feminine,
Neither god,
Nor the devil.

An instrument,
Of Astonishment,
And different.

Would you show the world'?
Would you be yourself for it?

would you be one side,
And not the other?

Watching mankind,
Standing, fighting, falling.

Imagine yourself in mythical glory;
As an angel;
Standing on a precipice,
not wanting to name the fallen.

Fear to blame

You have me by the hand,
You have me by the strings,
You wet my palms,
but exciting is your charm.

Shaking;
Voice croaking;
and breaking nervously.

Focus;
I tell myself,
because;
Fear;
I;
can't,
let,
you,
win.

Head swimming,
Vision blurry,
Chest with its own bass,
Da Dum
Da Dum
Da Dum
Shaking my body

And Paling my face.

Breaking the placid metronome,
The Tempo in my rib cage,
Shrilling from treble to deep dark bass;

Doom
Doom
Doom.

Fear,
to blame.

Die Pad

Anxiety rising,
Snatching breath from lungs,
Trying to draw in deep.
Heart pounding and racing,
Erratically and menacingly,
Messaging,
Run, run, run.
The mob is shouting,
Muscling in and shoving,
Singing and ululating loudly.

The police stand by,
Sirens and lights,
Blue, red and white,
Ready shields lined in fight,
Batons, the battle cry,
Rubber bullet armed,
Tear gas canisters pop,
And land in the crowds.
The ululating grows louder.

Pickets and signs;
A proud and pride town,
eyes wild and wide,
Sounds of violence,
Spreading like a virus,

The sentence,
Across every satellite.

DANCING WITH YOU

Dancing with you in a chair,
round and round without a care,
Dancing with you in a chair,
Pen and pad nodding your head,
Pen and pad nodding to the dead,
Just cash to you, could be dead,
Just cash to you, you must be dead.

Sirens and asylums, no shoes,
Padded walls, wearing straight jacket suits,
Paper cups, swallowing chewable untruth.
Shaking, waking, put to sleep again,
If I killed myself in front of you,
Would you lift your head?
Would you lift your head?

Pills, empty syringes, Valium,
Anti-psychotics, sleeping pills again,
Tranquilizers numbing my brain.
Nurses, doctors, locking cells,
Screaming, shouting, walls that melt,
A smile that can't be felt,
A smile that can't be felt.

Blister packs in school back packs,
Cold eyes looking up at a lecture stand,

Dead in a chair, with pen in hand.
Learning no one sees,
Learning no one cares,
Learning no one would know,
if I wasn't here.

Looking in the mirror at me,
Not what they say they see,
Not the person they want me to be.
Lost and looking at lies perceived,
Falling into an abyss of misery,
Where was the hand I needed?
To help me, to help me?

PARASITIC LOVE

Kiss me for a card,
Kiss me hard,
Slap your hand away,
Unless you pay, pay, pay,
Parasitic love,
Hidden within faked gush,
Parasitic love, uh-huh,
Parasitic love, uh-huh

Tell me what you want,
Tell me I can't,
Parasitic love, parasitic love,
Tell me What I am,
Tell me, I don't give a damn,
Parasitic love, parasitic love.
Hold me tight,
Throw a fist in a fight,
Parasitic love, parasitic love,
Tell me I am the only one,
Tell me I am your love,
Parasitic love, parasitic love.

Stand by my side,
Don't let me see your cheating eyes,
Parasitic love, parasitic love,
Tell me I am the best,

Place your head upon my chest,
Parasitic love, parasitic love.

Look into my eyes,
Tell me no lies,
Parasitic love, parasitic love,
Tell me I am your life,
Tell me tonight,
Parasitic love, parasitic love.

LONER KIDS

Do You know our strangeness?
You see us in strange places,
Do You know our weird looks?
You've seen our fuck offs,
The loner kids, the loner kids
The loner kids, the loner kids,
The loudest are the loner kids,
No one listens like the loner kids,
we are the loner kids
We are the loner kids.

Kick me to the dirt,
Push me, grab me by my shirt,
I will show you the loner kids,
I will show you the loner kids,
Lie to my face,
Take my heart, break it,
I will show you the loner kids,
I will show you the loner kids.

Do it all again, say that I will pay,
Take it all away,
I will show you the loner kids,
I will show you the loner kids.
Slap my face,
Twist my arm behind my back,

I will show you the loner kids,
I will show you the loner kids.

Tell me I am not worth it,
Laugh and laugh,
I will show you the loner kids,
I will show you the loner kids
Make me feel worthless,
Mock me, do it again,
I will show you the loner kids,
I will show you the loner kids.

MRS LABEL AND MR PRETEND

Mrs Label and Mr Pretend, UH!
It don't bother me, who-A!
She ain't worth it, who-A!
lipstick blowjobs and woe, UH!
Mrs I said so, uh
EVERYONE KNOWS, uh
EVERYONE KNOWS, uh
MRS LABEL AND MR PRETEND, who-UH!
MRS LABEL AND MR PRETEND, who-UH!

Wear Tight jeans, styled hair,
Mrs label and Mr pretend, uh
Gold chains, silicone fails,
Masks and Botox jails,
Air kisses and bought taste, uh
Acquaintances and associates, yea
Mrs label and Mr pretend,
EVERYONE KNOWS, uh
MRS LABEL AND MR PRETEND - UH!

Expensive dinners,
Expensive mess, UH!
Mrs label and Mr pretend, UH!
Acquaintances and associates,
Mr and Mrs pretend's friends, uh
Mrs label and Mr pretend, UH!

DIAMOND RINGS, uh
LOTS OF BLING, uh
MRS LABEL AND MR PRETEND- UH!

24 carrots, princess cut, UH
Loui Viton, strut your stuff,
Mrs label and Mr Pretend, UH!
Wear what they tell you to wear, UH
Designer t, marked up jeans,
Mrs Label and Mr Pretend, UH
THEY DON'T HAVE FRIENDS, UH
THEY HAVE "friends", uh
MRS LABEL AND MR PRETEND – uh!

Social climbers, up those stairs,
Pose, curtsy, wave, Botox glare, UH
Mrs Label and Mr Pretend
Don't even know who you are killing, UH
Little kids, sweat shop milling, UH
Mrs label and Mr Pretend-uh!
THEY WEAR WHAT THEY ARE TOLD TO WEAR, UH!
THEY POSE AND CURTSY AND DON'T CARE, UH!
MRS LABEL AND MR PRETEND, YEA!

KISS YOU

You ripped me open,
You left me dying,
Walked away,
Not even crying.
I am coming to kiss you,
You kneel before I do.
I am coming to kiss you,
You kneel before I do.

A love denied,
A love be cried,
A new demise,
A new lie,
I am coming to kiss you,
I am coming to kiss you.

A new mask,
A new face,
An old dress,
Made of black lace,
I am coming to kiss you,
I am coming to kiss you.

A new way,
The same race,
An omen made,

A sign gave,
I am coming to kiss you,
I am coming to kiss you

Goodbye today
The rites are paid,
I am coming to kiss you
I am coming to kiss you

eX-PeRI-MeNTAL-
WRITINg

A summit of sonnets, and an ode to the oval office,

              Do, or count, or compare, or fare yourself in relation to, someone who could never achieve your achievements, because of not having faced the same adversities,

              Nor allowed the same opportunities.

Should it be warranted that a political execution should take place, due to the dishonorable actions of one man;

              Then that man should not stand among us, that man should not be deemed fit to be one of us, because of his lack of respect for human life.

No woe sits upon the shoulders of those that are not concerned enough to acknowledge those men around them; that those men are in fact equal to them.

              The fact of refusal in acknowledgement, is the finest indication of how those possessing egos surmounting those of the lesser man,

are in fact lesser than the
man they believe to be less.

Relating to a desperate compulsion towards punctuality;

I ask from those that are
fluent in the vernacular, to address such queries,

and
concerns to the aforementioned distribution operator.

If you can sleep when the sun is shining;
If you can breathe when trees are dying,

if you can eat when you
know children are starving,

then you died long before now,

and the heart beating,

in your chest,

is a deception.

Flickering memories;
Images of pain,
Sights seen,
By times face.
Tugging at heartache,
Pulling it by the arm in dismay,
Cheater of death,
Playing a chicken game,
Fighting through every fear;
Until not one remains.

From the east and from the west;
The sky lights up,
Three powers;
A triumpherate;
The contenders,
The dominant players,
Sinking the united;
The fighters.

Upon a hill, upon a threat to kill
Raise your hands to your hearts,
Pledge your allegiance,
It's going to start raining bloody stars.

Printed in the United States
By Bookmasters